MARRIAGE AND THE FAMILY:
GOD'S PURPOSE AND PLAN

MARRIAGE AND THE FAMILY:
GOD'S PURPOSE AND PLAN
Greg Laurie

A publication of

>|< harvest: greg laurie

Riverside, California
www.harvest.org

Greg Laurie is senior pastor of Harvest Christian Fellowship in Riverside, California.

Marriage and the Family: God's Purpose and Plan

Text Copyright © 2004 by Harvest Ministries. All rights reserved.

Design: David Riley+Associates
Typesetting: Harvest Design
Copywriting: Harvest Publications
Copyediting: Harvest Publications

Originally published as *God's Blueprint for Today's Family*
Text Copyright © 1992 by Harvest Ministries

Printed in the United States of America.

ISBN: 1-932778-06-3

www.harvest.org

Contents

Preface:
Marriage under Attack

Hardly a day goes by in which I don't pick up the newspaper or turn on the television and hear of another attack on the family. Without question, this attack is wreaking havoc on our country, because the breakdown of the family directly affects our society as a whole.

On all fronts, it seems we have moved away from the purpose and plan God gave us from the very beginning. Yet this purpose and plan is not open to us to edit or play with or change. The family is the foundation of our very culture and civilization.

The big question is, "Are we going to live according to the teaching of God's Word?" Or, "Are we going to let this world squeeze us into its mold?"

It often seems like every group wants to participate in marriage but those for whom it was created can't carry out their commitment. God has told us what steps we need to take to have strong, successful, and yes, happy marriages, and He is clear on His purpose and plan.

As a pastor, I've counseled a large number of married couples over the years. I have observed that in every situation where a marriage is falling apart, there never has been an instance in which the husband and wife were simply doing what God's Word told them. Somehow, they thought they were the exception to the rule: "Well, I know the Bible says this, but you see, my case is different."

I speak a little more passionately about marriage and the family than others might, because I am the product of a broken home. My mom married and divorced seven times. I know what it's like to live in a broken home. I know what it's like not to have both of my parents. I know what it's like to see what happens when a family doesn't stay together.

Maybe you have really tried to make your marriage work, but things have been rough. I want to ask, have you gone back to what the Scripture teaches and really applied those biblical principles? God has given us bedrock principles that we can apply and make our marriages not only succeed, but blessed, happy, and fulfilling.

Here at Harvest Ministries, we want to offer hope and encouragement for every area of your life through the teaching of God's Word. We are interested in strengthening the family by helping husbands love their wives, helping wives love their husbands, helping parents raise their children, and helping the family stay strong.

That is why I've written this book, *Marriage and the Family: God's Purpose and Plan*. I wrote it to help you understand what the Bible says about marriage and see God's original blueprint for marriage and the family. Even if you have a strong marriage, this booklet will help make it stronger. It also offers some helpful words of wisdom to those who are not yet married but hope to be some day.

It has been said that a family can survive without a country, but a country cannot survive without the family. If you're married, I want to encourage you today to draw the line and take a stand by committing to make your marriage work—God's way. God wants to bless your marriage so that it not only survives, but also thrives and is an example for all to see what He has created.

Chapter One:
God's Purpose for Marriage

Sometimes we hear the phrase, "They have a marriage made in heaven." And of course, the flip side of that phrase is, "They have a marriage made in hell." Comments such as these reveal the trouble with marriages today. Too many people think that good marriages simply fall from the sky, while bad marriages creep up from below. What they don't realize is that good marriages are founded upon hard work, commitment, love, and most importantly—obedience to God's Word.

Jesus said, "Anyone who listens to my teaching and obeys me is wise, like a person who builds a house on solid rock" (Matthew 7:24 NLT). Now apply this to marriage. When you build your marriage upon the Word of God, you're building it upon a solid rock. Your marriage will be firm in Jesus—the solid Rock—when all the turmoil, all the stress, and all the problems come your way.

In the book of Genesis, God provides us with His

purpose for marriage. We read in Genesis 2, "Therefore a man shall leave his father and mother and be joined to his wife, and they shall become one flesh" (2:24). God's purpose for marriage was companionship and for a husband and wife to unite together as one. This is the essence of a marriage built upon the Word of God. It consists of two core principles: leaving and cleaving.

Every good marriage begins with leaving. Leaving is the act of altering all other relationships in your life. Besides your relationship with God, your relationship with your spouse becomes the relationship of priority. According to Genesis 2:24, if it's necessary to leave your father and mother, then certainly all lesser relationships must be broken, changed, or left behind. There are far too many marriages on the rocks because of unbiblical priorities. If you're closer to another person than you are to your spouse, then you need to make a change! You need to replace the guys' or girls' night out with a date night with your spouse.

Some of you may think you have this part nailed. But let me ask you, what about your career? Is your career more important than your spouse? Do you put in more overtime at the office than you do at home? Is advancing in the work place more important than advancing your relationship with your spouse? If so, then it's time to redirect and get back to God's purpose for marriage.

Make your spouse number one in your life. The husband's primary commitment must be to his wife and the wife's primary commitment must be to her husband.

This is what the Bible calls "cleaving." The word *cleaving* means to cement together, to stick like glue, or to be welded together so the two cannot be separated without serious damage to both. In other words, you and your spouse are friends—best friends.

This commitment begins with becoming one. God's purpose for your marriage is that you be one flesh. A husband and wife are to be so closely woven together physically, emotionally, and spiritually that you are not to be a whole person apart from each other. Does that describe your marriage?

To keep our marriages godly and strong, we must periodically ask ourselves, "Are we doing what it takes to strengthen our marriage? Are we engaged in any relationship or in any pursuit that could potentially put distance between us? Will this thing that we are engaged in right now build up our relationship or tear it down? Are we leaving and cleaving?" Remember that marriage is based first and foremost on God, friendship, closeness, and intimacy.

Does your marriage need to be rekindled? Then rekindle that fire in your relationship. Saying you can't is like sitting down in front of the fireplace, and when the fire begins to die down, you say, "That's it! The fire is gone. We will never have another fire again. It was a great fire at one time. But now I guess it's time to get a new house and a new fireplace." No one ever says that. So throw another log on the fire. It will burn again. Likewise, throw another log on the fire of your marriage and watch it come back to life. The first step to a rekindled marriage is a marriage founded upon the Word of God. Open up God's instruction manual and watch your relationship with your spouse transform.

Chapter Two:
God's Plan for Marriage

In the fifth chapter of Ephesians, we find an excellent exposition on Christian marriage and the foundation upon which to build it. The Apostle Paul states, "Wives, submit to your own husbands, as to the Lord" (Ephesians 5:22). Husbands will often quote that verse to their wives. Similarly, wives often quote to their husbands the familiar verse, "Husbands, love your wives, just as Christ also loved the church and gave Himself for her" (Ephesians 5:25). But to fully understand these verses, we need to look at the verses that lead into this definitive passage on marriage, and the specific roles of the husband and the wife. With that in mind, let's look at the fifth chapter of Ephesians to shed some light on this often misunderstood territory called "marriage."

Let God's Light Expose Problem Areas

Addressing the believers in Ephesus, the Apostle Paul wrote, "But all things that are exposed are made manifest by the light, for whatever makes manifest is light" (Ephesians 5:13). The phrase "make manifest," literally means "to make visible something which has previously been hidden." In other words, when God's light shines on something, it exposes the problem. The psalmist, recognizing this truth, said, "Your word is a lamp to my feet and a light to my path" (Psalm 119:105). We also have the assurance from Jesus, who said, "I am the light of the world" (John 8:12). If we will address our marriages as Jesus and the Word of God direct us, then we will be guided back to the path of stability and safety from which we've strayed. When the Holy Spirit speaks to our hearts, we see the areas of our life that need to be corrected. It must be understood that before we can be of any help in our family, before we can find recovery, we must first, as individuals, admit that we've strayed from God's original plan. We all need to recognize that we have room for improvement.

If you have built your marriage on a biblical foundation from the start, then you will have a blessed and successful marriage. On the other hand, if you've been married for a while, and the whole thing is beginning to crumble, it is most likely that you have built upon a faulty foundation. Although it is always harder to correct or to repair something than to have done it right from the beginning, it is still possible. If you have ever remodeled your home, you know how difficult that can be. But whatever it takes, whatever needs to be torn up, repaired, or replaced, it's simply got to be done. The same is true in a faltering marriage. In order to build a godly marriage you must let God's light shine in and help to identify the problems. Then you must address those problems one by one and solve them.

Turn from the World's Ways to God's Ways

Equipped with Christ's light and guidance, building a godly marriage involves awaking from a dying or mediocre marriage, and forsaking what the ways of the world have taught you. As Paul said, "Awake, you who sleep, arise from the dead, and Christ will give you light" (Ephesians 5:14). The second chapter of Ephesians really sums up the whole world system, as well as our old lives before we know Christ. It says that in the past, we all drifted along the stream of the world's idea of living.

Place God's Plan before Your Own

God's plan for a godly marriage requires that you get rid of the mindset that seeks self-gratification and personal gain, and to replace it with one that seeks God's will above all else. Equipped with this attitude, we will see that it is more important to be in the will of God than to be "happy," particularly if we seek what the world calls happiness. Happiness can be a deceptive pursuit, a masquerade deceiving us with the pleasure of sin. If feelings of happiness or positive emotions gauge as to whether or not you are in the place you want to be, I guarantee you will find yourself in trouble. First and foremost, we must pursue the perfect will of God to be where He wants us. Interestingly enough, in doing so, we will find that we are, indeed, happy. Happiness is only a by-product. If I pursue happiness as my number one goal, then I can very easily be diverted and wind up empty. Instead, we must get away from that "me first" thinking, and think of God, His will, and our mate.

Marriage is not so much finding the right person, as it

is being the right person. Actually, when we take our eyes off ourselves and place them on our spouse, we often find the happiness we've been looking for. Once we awake and realize this fact, Paul tells us that we must learn to walk circumspectly (see Ephesians 5:15). To walk circumspectly means to be constantly taking heed of our conduct. Another way to put it is, "to keep your eyes on the road." Personally, I struggle with this at times. If I have to drive a long stretch, especially on the freeway, I'll often begin fiddling with things like my glove compartment or start playing with the radio. I'll essentially do anything to break the monotony. But I'll immediately know I'm going astray when I hear that awful thumping of my tires on those little bumps, reminding me to get back in line.

In the same way, we've got to get our eyes back on God's road, and keep them there. We need to walk circumspectly. God has specific orders for the husband and for the wife, but too often I hear us quoting the verses to each other instead of taking heed of them ourselves! This is no different than going out to the mailbox and reading through your wife's mail. It all boils down to this: a man and a woman must read their own mail! Husbands, are you loving your wives as yourselves (see Ephesians 5:33)? Wives, are you respecting your husbands (see Ephesians 5:33)? If we are willing to do so, this will be the turning point in our marriages. Before either of those objectives can be met, however, we need to take a few more important steps.

Understand God's Design for Marriage
Paul says, in Ephesians 5:15–17, not to act "as fools

but as wise, redeeming the time, because the days are evil. Therefore, do not be unwise, but understand what the will of the Lord is." Remember the story Jesus told about the wise man who built his house upon the rock (see Matthew 7:24–27)? When the storms and rains came and beat upon his house, it stood firm because it was on a foundation of rock. The foolish man built his house upon the sand, and when the same elements beat against this man's marriage, it fell because it was on a foundation of sand. Marriage is like that house. What you're building a marriage on determines its ability to stand. Essentially, Jesus was saying, "The wise man is he who hears the Word of God and does it, while the foolish man is he who hears the Word of God and does it not."

If you are hearing what God says, as well as doing what God says, then the Lord sees you as being wise. The same storms that destroy other marriages will not destroy yours, but will actually solidify and strengthen it. On the other hand, if you're not doing what God says, that same storm will devastate your marriage. Marriages fall apart today because couples do not follow God's plan for them.

I've yet to counsel a couple that was separated or considering divorce in which the husband loved his wife as Christ loved the church, and the wife submitted to her husband as unto the Lord. Never! The common reply is usually, "Yeah, well, that Bible stuff is okay for some, but it won't help my situation." Why don't we just do what God tells us to do! It seems, admittedly, too simplistic, yet I've seen the results time and again. If we channel our energies into what God says, He'll take care of the rest. If we seek first His kingdom, which means His Lordship in our lives and our marriages, all of those problem areas in marriage will fall into place.

Sadly, our refusal to be wise in this area has created the tremendously high divorce rate we have today. Some argue, "Well, we just have a bad marriage." They often conclude this thought by saying, "I wish we had a good marriage like other couples, but we just have a bad one." Such thinking is ludicrous. Marriage is what you make it. If it's a good marriage, it's because two people have worked at making it good. If it's a bad marriage, it's because two people have worked at making it bad.

Marriage is like a mirror. It just reflects what it sees. Next to my bed at home stands a mirror. When I sit up in the morning, the first thing I see is myself. I don't like that. I look like death warmed over in the morning. But you see, it's not the mirror's fault. It just reflects what it sees. To replace that mirror with a new one makes about as much sense as trading in one marriage for another. The problems won't disappear. There are countless numbers of people who have dissolved a marriage only to start a new relationship and find that they're faced with the very same set of problems, plus a few new ones they never expected. The grass is not greener on the other side.

You Cannot Build a Good Marriage on Your Own

Paul continues his teaching in Ephesians by saying, "And do not be drunk with wine, in which is dissipation;

but be filled with the Spirit" (5:18). In the original language, this is not a suggestion; it is an imperative. In other words, it's a command. We need the Holy Spirit operating in our lives. Before a Christian marriage can succeed, both parties must realize they cannot do it in their own strength. I've heard couples say that they've really tried, but the marriage just won't work. They are convinced there is no hope for the marriage. Good! I want to hear them say that. I want them to admit they have tried everything. It's at this time they realize they cannot do it in their own ability. There is an old saying, "When we get to the end of ourselves, we get to the beginning of God."

So what does it mean to be filled with the Spirit? Is it some euphoric, emotional state that comes over us and suddenly takes all control? Not exactly. To be filled with the Spirit means that you're living a Spirit-controlled life, that you're letting God's Spirit help you be the woman or man He's called you to be. It is to be filled with God, His Word, His power, and to be emptied of ourselves.

Submission: the Most Neglected and Abused Marriage Ingredient

Submission is not a word people like to hear too often—especially with the current feminist movement. The Bible plainly says, "submit to one another out of reverence for Christ" (Ephesians 5:21 NLT). When God said that Christians should submit to one another, and when He assigned submission as a primary role of the woman, He did not mean that women were to become a doormat for men. If anything, God liberated the woman.

In the time that Paul wrote his epistle to the Ephesians, society treated the woman as a second-class citizen, something more akin to a possession. A conversation between most men of that day probably went something like, "Yeah, I have five cows, three barns, and a wife." The woman was nothing more than a possession.

Paul refuted this type of thinking by commanding the man to "love your wife as Christ loves the church." The men must have thought Paul had lost his mind! To love a wife like Jesus loved the church meant to love her sacrificially. Incidentally, in all the marriage counseling I have performed, I've never heard a wife complain that her husband loved her too much. Unfortunately, that somehow never happens.

Before defining the woman's role of submission in verse 22, Paul makes it a point in verse 21 to remind both men and women to "submit to one another out of reverence for Christ." To put this teaching of submission in context, we must know that all Christians, husbands and wives included, must submit to one another.

What then does this word *submit* really mean? The word actually means to "respond to" or "adapt to." That's exactly what marriage is. It's adapting and responding one to another. The truth of the matter is that the word in this context has a meaning of voluntary submission. Therefore, one Christian can't tell or force another Christian to submit. If they do, it isn't submission—it's oppression. How does that apply to marriage? In marriage, submission is something that a spouse— husband or wife—willingly chooses to do in obedience to Christ. After all, if you have to make your spouse submit to you, then it's no longer biblical submission— it's worldly and ungodly (see Matthew 20:25–28; Mark 10:42–45).

The Mystery of Marriage

In the beginning, God created man. He then made woman because he realized "It is not good that man should be alone" (Genesis 2:18). So as Adam went to sleep, God took one of his ribs and made woman. When Adam awoke, he responded, "This is now bone of my bones and flesh of my flesh; she shall be called Woman, because she was taken out of Man" (Genesis 2:23). From this came the old Hebrew proverb that says, "Woman wasn't made from a man's head to be above him, nor from a man's feet to be walked upon by him, but from his rib to be close to his heart."

From that passage in Genesis, we also find a verse that should already be familiar to us: "Therefore a man shall leave his father and mother and be joined to his wife, and they shall become one flesh" (Genesis 2:24 KJV). Later in this chapter of Ephesians, Paul quotes that same passage from Genesis. He refers to the "becoming one flesh" as a mystery. It remains somewhat of a mystery today. God, the creator of marriage, supernaturally "bonds" together a Christian husband and wife.

Now, in all marriages—even good ones—there will be differences of opinion and characteristics. In fact, it's been said that opposites attract. I know it's that way in my marriage. My wife and I are very different from one another. That's one of the things that originally attracted me to her. I did not want to marry someone like me. I have enough of me. I wanted someone else. But it is interesting how we pick up the traits of our opposites and incorporate them into our own character.

I have a strange habit that my wife has picked up. You see, I don't like to stand still when I brush my teeth. I'll be brushing, and then I'll start walking around the house and do other things. Some time ago, I noticed my wife had started doing it. We'll be brushing somewhere in the house and suddenly bump into each other. To an outsider this must appear somewhat comical; nonetheless, it is just one of the many ways in which we have become "one flesh."

A Word of Caution to Singles

I caution singles who misinterpret what it means to become "one flesh." If you, as a single Christian today, are falling head over heels for a nonbeliever with the idea of changing that person after getting married, watch out. Throw on the brakes. As Benjamin Franklin said, "Keep your eyes wide open before marriage and half shut afterwards." That other person just may not change. In fact, I hate to say this, but he or she may get worse.

A Christian has no business pursuing a relationship with a nonbeliever. Disaster usually follows, and the Bible forbids it (see 2 Corinthians 6:14). Rather, both parties had better be more concerned with conforming to God's image. That involves coming together under God's authority. Then when you're married, it involves becoming fused together into one flesh. This bonding takes a lifetime, and that is why God's Word warns believers against being "unequally yoked" with nonbelievers in marriage.

Desire to Make Your Marriage Pleasing to Jesus

In what light should I respond and adapt to my mate? Paul tells us to respond "in the fear of Christ" (Ephesians 5:21 ASV). According to *Vine's Expository Dictionary of New Testament Words*, the phrase, "fear Christ" can be translated, "A reverential fear, of God, as a controlling motive of the life . . . ."[1] It is more than just a fear of His power and righteous retribution. It's a wholesome dread of displeasing Him.

My desire is to have a marriage that is pleasing to Jesus. I want to do it His way. I have a fear, not of being punished were my marriage to come apart, but rather of bringing sorrow to God's heart by neglecting my marital responsibilities. That brings shame to Him, and I don't want that to happen. Out of reverence and devotion to God, I want my marriage to be pleasing to Him. This is an important concept to remember.

View Your Marriage As a Representation of Christ and the Church

The marriage relationship is unique in that God has especially chosen it to be the physical representation of His relationship with the church. The Apostle Paul said, "Wives, submit to your own husbands, as to the Lord" (Ephesians 5:22), and "Husbands, love your wives, just as Christ also loved the church . . . ." (Ephesians 5:25). In seeing the way a husband loves his wife, and the way a wife responds to her husband, we see, in a miniature form, the relationship between Christ and the church.

Our marriages are a witness for Christ. Like it or not, we are either a good or a bad witness. If your marriage is struggling today, if you are having problems today, I want you to rule out one thought. Whatever it takes, rule out dissolving your marriage. As Winston Churchill said, "Victory is not won by evacuation." Victory is never won by running out and saying, "It's too hard. I'm getting out of here." You can make it, but you've got to get back to God's ideal, and you've got to do it God's way.

A godly marriage involves looking at what God has said to you, and then trusting God to deal with your spouse. Are you willing to do that? Are you willing to do some remodeling? Come back to God's ideal and let Him fill you with the power of His Spirit. Be that wise man or woman who practices what God has set forth in His Word. Then, when the storms of life come (and they will), your marriage, built upon the Rock, will stand.

Chapter Three:
God's Purpose and Plan for the Family

Satan has declared war on the family! From the beginning of time, God's plan has always been to build, strengthen, and protect the family. Satan's plan, on the other hand, has been to undermine, weaken, and destroy it. I believe that the various attempts we see to undermine the family in today's society are satanic in origin. You will find that the majority of our problems today stem from either a broken home or a home in which biblical principles were ignored or disobeyed.

God's Word on Children

Respect for parents is certainly a biblical principle we have lost sight of in our culture. It is interesting to note that the Bible identifies disobedience as one of the signs of the last days. The Apostle Paul makes this clear in his letter to Timothy, where he says, "In the last days men will be lovers of themselves, lovers of money, boasters, proud, blasphemers, without natural affection, and *disobedient to parents*" (2 Timothy 3:2, emphasis mine).

When you look at our culture today, a lack of respect

and an abundance of disobedience is clearly evident in children. Our secular culture is a monolith of rebellion against godly principles. Television sitcoms routinely portray parents and especially fathers as blithering idiots. The children on the other hand are depicted as all-knowing personalities who are full of scripted wisecracks, no doubt, penned by adults who never really grew up themselves.

Consider the fact that today's average child watches thirty hours of television per week. Before graduating from high school, the typical American teenager will have watched twenty thousand hours of television. What is even more discouraging, the majority of programs, which a child will have watched, portrays authority figures as evil and rebellion as a virtue. Your children will see sin glamorized and homosexuality presented as not only acceptable but as an avenue young people should explore. Ultimately, the typical child's and young adult's total television-viewing experience will represent immorality as morality.

I think that you will agree with me that this viewpoint on Hollywood is not mere hyperbole on my part. It is a simple fact that most of Hollywood has a way of glamorizing sin. They make it look good. You can sit in a film that is blatantly contradicting your biblical values and secretly find yourself rooting for something or someone due to the fact that the movie's direction, acting, and cinematography present sin in an attractive manner.

Simply put, the world's influence on our children is

frightening. That's why it is imperative that we know God's Word for the family, which Paul provides in Ephesians 6. Let's look at it together. "Children, obey your parents in the Lord, for this is right. 'Honor your father and mother,' which is the first commandment with promise: 'that it may be well with you and you may live long on the earth' " (Ephesians 6:1–2). Paul echoes this same idea over in Colossians 3:20 when he says, "Children, obey your parents in all things, for this is well pleasing to the Lord."

God has given parents and children these commandments as a set of moral absolutes by which to live. In a culture that increasingly embraces moral relativism, it is essential that we return to the Scriptures to discover what is right and wrong. This obviously flies against the cultural bias of today. Nowadays we hear more about children's rights than we do about their responsibilities. Kids are not only expected to rebel, they are encouraged to rebel. This is not God's order.

What is worse is that many times parents give into unbiblical principles. Some Christian parents believe that once their children are in their teens, they don't need parenting anymore. This is a grave error. They need you more than ever. Even into their adult years your influence continues.

There is an interesting little twist on this command for children to honor and obey their parents, which comes out in the original language. The Greek word translated *children* in Ephesians 6 is a broad term that applies to adult offspring as well as young toddlers. This means that the influence and training of parents toward their children continues throughout life. God's design ultimately is that a man leaves his father and mother and is joined unto his wife and the two become one flesh. But even when that happens, there is always to be a respect and honor on the part of the children toward their parents.

Paul reminds children and parents that this command to honor and obey parents is followed by a promise, "that it may be well with you and you may live long on the earth" (Ephesians 6:3). There are two aspects to that promise. First, that it may be well with you. This aspect promises a quality of life to children who honor and obey their parents. The second aspect is that you may live long on earth. This guarantees a quantity of life. The fact of the matter is that children who honor their parents tend to live longer and fuller lives than those who do not. This is because they are in God's order.

Sadly, many children do not honor their parents simply because many parents are not very honorable. Many adults never grow up themselves. They abandon the responsibilities of a family to chase after whatever it is that will make them happy. As a parent, you must realize that God has placed you as the authority in the life of the child. In many ways, parents represent God to their children.

I once heard a story about a little boy who was frightened one night by a very loud thunderstorm. He called out to his father in the next room, "Daddy, I'm scared!" But the dad didn't really want to get out of bed.

He said, "Son, don't be scared. God is with you." The boy paused for a moment then said; "Yeah, but I want someone with skin on!"

Parents, in many ways your children see you as God with skin on. I don't mean that literally—but you are the representative of God to your child. Think about this. Many of the attitudes that your child will develop about God will be based on their relationship with you. This is why we need to do everything we can to be a godly influence upon our children. When your little kids, even as they get older, see you and your spouse contradicting what you know is true, you inflict great damage on them. That is why Andrew Murray said, "The secret of home rule is self rule. First being ourselves what we want our children to be."

Our children must see the gospel lived as well as preached in our lives. Parents need to live as witnesses to the outside world, as well as witnesses in their home. Little eyes are watching and little ears are listening. Your children are paying attention to what really matters to you and how your faith affects you in day-to-day living.

Moms and dads, listen to me. As I previously said, you are an example. The question is, "Are you going to be a good one or a bad one."

God's Word to Parents
Looking at our world today, how can we deny that we are not living in satanically energized times? Our children face unparalleled pressures today. Teenage

suicide has reached epidemic levels as never before in history. While conducting research for this book, I found one common link in every major problem facing our culture. That link was the disintegration of the family. Whether the problem was drug abuse, teenage pregnancy, violent crimes, gang activity, teenage suicide, or homosexuality, it seemed that children in trouble usually came from broken homes or homes where the mother and father were neglecting the children because they were too busy with other things.

Sadly, many children are being left alone without a father or a mother to guide them. Proverbs 29:15 says, "a child left to himself brings shame to his mother." Why is that? Proverbs 22:15 explains that it's because "Foolishness is bound up in the heart of a child." The truth is that children left without the proper parental care will wind up pursuing foolish endeavors. Today's world is a testimony to this biblical truth.

Author Kay S. Hymowitz testifies to this truth in her *Wall Street Journal* article entitled, "Kids Today Grow up Way Too Fast." Hymowitz's article focuses on children between the ages of eight and twelve years of age, which she says marketers are dubbing "tweens." She points out that, "Tweening of childhood is more than just a matter of fashion. Tweens are demonstrating many of the deviant behaviors we usually associate with adolescence."[1] What is interesting is that Hymowitz's findings reveal that the cause of deviant behavior in tweens is due to absentee parents and sexually driven marketing. She states,

In my conversations with educators and child psychologists who work primarily with middle-class kids nationwide, two major and fairly predictable themes emerged: absentee parents and a sexualized and glitzy media-driven marketplace. What has been less commonly recognized is the way these two influences combine to augment the authority of the peer group. With their parents working long hours away from home, many youngsters are leaving for school from an empty house after eating breakfast alone, then picking up fast food or frozen meals for dinner. Almost without exception, the principals and teachers I spoke with describe a pervasive loneliness among tweens. "The most common complaint I hear," says Ms. Hogan, "is 'My mom doesn't care what I do. She's never home. She doesn't even know what I do.' "[2]

This article substantiates that time and again good parenting comes down to quantity time—not just quality time. Despite this biblical truth, parents place their careers or other interests over the needs of their children. The truth of the matter is that the little time many parents do spend with their children far from qualifies as quality time. All too often, a vast majority of parents model unbiblical and even immoral behavior during the short time they spend with their children. According to Dr. David Elkind's book *The Hurried Child: Growing up Too Fast Too Soon*, it has been recognized that the negative changes in America's teenagers are merely "mirror shifts of adult society."[3] In other words, teenagers mirror what they see in adults. Indeed, adults today are more sexually permissive, tolerant of drug and alcohol use, and swayed by materialism, and this generation's youth are following in their footsteps. It is then no wonder why people like Kay Hymowitz are finding such troubling results within the family and especially within today's children.

I believe children today are looking for absolutes. They may act like they don't want them, but in reality they do. In his address to fathers in Ephesians chapter six, Paul lays out some specific directives for parents. Though he specifically addresses fathers, these principles are applicable to mothers, as well. Paul says, "fathers, do not provoke your children to wrath" (Ephesians 6:4). This is an interesting phrase. Another way to translate this is "Fathers, don't exasperate your children." It also implies that parents should never enrage, irritate, harass, or add fuel to the flame when dealing with their children.

This same thought is echoed in Colossians 3:21 where Paul says, "Do not provoke your children, lest they become discouraged." Here, the word *discouraged* is added, which could be better translated, "lest they have their spirits broken."

Show Each Child Equal Affection

A parent can break the spirit of a child in many ways. One way is by showing favoritism to one child over another. This happened with Isaac and Rebekah and their two sons Jacob and Esau (see Genesis 27). Isaac favored Esau, while Rebekah favored Jacob. As a result, a wedge was hammered into the relationship of Jacob and Esau that later became a great conflict. As a parent, you must prayerfully plan and strive to treat your children equally.

Encourage Your Child

Another way you can provoke a child is by discouragement. A child whom a parent never compliments or encourages is bound for trouble. If a child is only told what is wrong with him or her and never what is right, that child will soon lose hope and become convinced he or she is incapable of doing anything right. By the time the average child enters kindergarten, he or she has heard the word *no* over forty thousand times. Certainly children need to be told "no," but they also need to be praised when they've done well.

Spiritually Train Your Child

The Apostle Paul tells parents to "bring them [their children] up in the training and admonition of the Lord" (Ephesians 6:4). We are to train our children. What does that mean? A frequently quoted verse on the subject of training our children, Proverbs 22:6, says, "Teach your children to choose the right path, and when they are older, they will remain upon it" (NLT). I think this verse has been largely misunderstood. Many Christian parents cart their children off to church on Sunday mornings, enroll them in Christian schools, take them to Christian camps, and drill Scripture into their minds. After doing all they can, in their estimation, to make a Christian out of their child, the child one day rebels against God. The parents are left saying, "What went wrong? I raised them in the way of the Lord." But did they?

Create a Spiritual Thirst

What does it really mean to train up a child? In the original language, the phrase, "train up" was used to speak of the actions of a midwife, who, after a child was born, dipped her finger in crushed dates and placed it in the mouth of the infant. By doing this, she created a thirst for milk in the infant. In the same way, we are to create a thirst in our children for the things of God. The phrase "train up" speaks of breaking, as a trainer brings into submission a wild horse by putting a rope in its mouth. It conveys the idea of motivating internally, as well as providing external boundaries. Accordingly, we are to establish external boundaries for our children, but we must also create an internal thirst for God in their lives.

Keep Training up to Adulthood

As I mentioned earlier, the word *child* refers to children from infancy to young adulthood. That means as long as our children are under our care, we are to train them in the Lord. I think some parents tend to stop training when their children hit the teen years, but that may be when they need it the most.

Mold Them into God's Design, Not Your's

Next, we're told to train our children in the way they should go (see Ephesians 6:4). Note, Paul does not say we should lead them in the way we want them to go! Many parents try to live out their ambitions or fantasies through their children. This is wrong. Dads, your son may never be the next Billy Graham. Moms, your daughter may never be the next Elisabeth Elliot. Every child has his or her own bent or preprogrammed set of directions. It is our role as parents to understand the unique bent of our child and work with him or her accordingly. This may mean you'll have to discipline two different ways. The rules will be the same for both children, but the administration of discipline may differ due to their individual temperaments. What may be perfect for one child may break the spirit of another.

If we were to look at this entire statement in context, we could better translate it this way: "Create a thirst in, train up, and build into the child the experience of submission, and adapt that training so that in keeping with his or her God-given abilities and tendencies, he or she may come to maturity and not depart from the training he or she has received."

Maintain Your Spiritual Passion

In Deuteronomy 6:6–7, Moses gives us greater insight into the reason for training our children:

> And these words which I command you today shall be *in your heart*. You shall teach them diligently to your children, and shall talk of them when you sit in your house, when you walk by the way, when you lie down, and when you rise up. (emphasis mine)

Notice that Moses first says that these words of God must be fixed in the heart of the parent! Nothing of substance will ever happen through us until it has first happened to us. If you're having difficulty in bringing your children closer to Christ, it may be that you have cooled in your passion for Jesus.

Make Time for Your Child

In Deuteronomy 6:6–7, Moses teaches parents to make time for their children. Moses essentially says that we

are to teach God's values to our children all the time,
every where. We are to teach God's Word when we sit
down with our children, when we walk with them, and
when we lie down with them. Parents must teach God's
values constantly and with quality. Once again, I believe
we are being deceived by the concept of "quality time"
versus "quantity time." I think the notion of quality time
is a cop out for parents who are not facing up to their
responsibility. What does it mean to have quality time,
anyway? Children need to be around their parents to
see them in every situation. It is often in the midst of
quantity time that we stumble into great conversations
and times of teaching—whether it is in the car on the
way to the grocery store or at the dinner table. It is
nearly impossible to schedule profound, meaningful
conversations. Good talks occur as we spend time with
our children.

Make It a Way of Life

Lastly, Moses says we are to teach God's truths
diligently. This word *diligent* means "to sharpen." It
conveys the idea of one object piercing through another
object. In other words, the training we are to give to
our children is to penetrate. What we teach them should
pierce deeply into their heart. Parents aren't called
merely to provide a set of dos and don'ts. They are to
develop in their children a set of convictions that will
carry them through life.

If you find your child watching an offensive program on
television, it's not enough to simply tell him or her to
turn it off. This is an opportunity to instill values into
your child. Tell your son or daughter why that program

is not helpful, and why watching it is displeasing to Jesus. After all, our object is to bring our children to Christ, to have our Christian convictions become their convictions. I once heard about a parent whose son was listening to some distasteful music. He took his son's CD, pulled out the lyric sheet, and read it with his son as they listened carefully to the words and music. By doing that, he was able to show his child why he believed as he did. The greatest joy a parent can have is to see his or her children responding to God's truth. As John said, "I have no greater joy than to hear that my children walk in truth" (3 John 4).

Perhaps you're falling short as a parent today. Take the time to reevaluate. If you've been unfair, seek your child's forgiveness. For there is one thing in which we can usually be certain: even as God is ever ready and willing to forgive, most often our children are eager and willing to reestablish their relationship with us. Perhaps they need only see you make the first move. Humbling yourself before your children does not teach them weakness. It teaches them humility and submission. Those traits will take them a long, long way.

Ten Commandments for Parents from Kids with a Troubled Past

I read about a pastor who helped out at a correctional center one summer. The boys there had already gone through the system and had been in all sorts of trouble. This pastor set out to discover why these boys chose the course they did. He asked them to identify for him what some of the problems might have been and asked them to help him draw up a code for parents that zeroed in on specific areas where their parents had failed. Here is the list the boys came up with:

1. **Keep cool.** Don't fly off the handle. Keep the lid on when things are going wrong. Kids need to see how much better things turn out when people keep their tempers under control.

2. **Don't get strung out on booze or drugs.** When we see our parents reaching for these crutches, we get the idea that it is perfectly okay to reach for a bottle or a capsule when things get heavy. Children are great imitators.

3. **Bug us a little.** Be strict. Show us who is boss. We need to know we have some strong support under us. When you cave in, we get scared.

4. **Don't blow your class.** Stay on that pedestal. Don't try to dress, dance, or talk like your kids. You embarrass us and you look ridiculous.

5. **Light a candle.** Show us the way. God is not dead or sleeping or on vacation. We need to believe in something bigger and stronger than ourselves.

6. **Scare us.** If you catch us lying, stealing, or being cruel, get tough. Let us know why what we did was wrong. Impress on us the importance of not repeating such behavior.

7. **When we need punishment, dish it out.** But let us know you still love us even though we have let you down. It will make us think twice before we do that again.

8. **Call our bluff.** Make it clear you mean what you say. Don't compromise. Don't be intimidated by our threats to drop out of school or to run away from home. Stand up to us and we'll respect you. Kids don't want everything they ask for.

9. **Be honest.** Tell the truth no matter what. Be a straight arrow about everything. We can take it. Lukewarm answers make us uneasy. We can smell uncertainty a mile away.

10. **Praise us when we deserve it.** Give us a few compliments once in a while, and we will be able to accept criticism a whole lot easier.

Do you know what those boys were saying? They were asking their parents to be involved in their lives. They also were asking their parents to teach what the Bible teaches, because every item on their list is actually based on biblical principles. If you feel as though you've failed as a parent, take heart. Our God is a God of second chances. Take a moment to pray, asking God to help you, through His Holy Spirit, to be the godly parent He wants you to be. If you sincerely want to change, I can assure you that you have already made an important first step in that direction. It's my prayer that you will hold fast to the teachings in God's Word so that you may become "the pride of [your] children" (Proverbs 17:6 NIV).

Chapter Four
Learning to Live God's Word

The institution of marriage and the family is not falling to pieces due to God's purpose and plan. There is nothing wrong with the guidelines He has established for families to follow. It is our refusal to seek and apply God's purpose and plan that is causing more and more marriages to end in divorce. In its 2001 survey, The Barna Group noted that "33% of all born again individuals who have been married have gone through a divorce, which is statistically identical to the 34% incidence among non-born again adults."[1] Tragically, Barna's research shows that the divorce rate in the church is close to surpassing the divorce rate in the world. This has to stop. But until we, as Christians, learn to live God's Word, the divorce epidemic will only grow worse.

Sadly, most couples today treat their marriages and families like a man who is behind the wheel and is clearly lost. Despite the fact that he has no idea where he is and has little hope of finding the way home, he refuses to pull over and ask for directions. People can be stubborn that way. We can be the same way with our marriages. We'll say to ourselves, "I can figure out our problems on my own. I know how to make a marriage work. I know how to live my life." Actually, we don't know how. People are not built with these truths preprogrammed into their hearts and minds. We first must learn God's truths and then learn how to apply them to our marriages and families.

We need to understand that in the Bible, God has given us a handbook for living. It is God's very Word to His people. The Apostle Paul said this about the Word of God, "All Scripture is inspired by God and is useful to teach us what is true and to make us realize what is wrong in our lives. It straightens us out and teaches us to do what is right. It is God's way of preparing us in every way fully equipped for every good thing God wants us to do" (2 Timothy 3:16–17 NLT). We want to apply these principles from the Bible in marriage and the family so we can have our relationships with our spouse and children straightened out if need be and be fully equipped for the good things God desires us to accomplish. I believe that is possible.

Let me just say to you, if your marriage and family is struggling—it can be saved. But only God can heal it. That healing begins by surrendering your family to God. You need to learn to live God's Word through the help and power of the Holy Spirit. This is the only way you can see your family life turned around.

If while reading this book you have decided to draw the line and take a stand by committing to make your marriage work, then you now have made the most important marital decision of your life. It is also a decision and commitment that requires dedication to obeying God no matter what.

To put your dedication in action, be sure you and your spouse spend time together by reading the Bible, praying, going to church, and telling others about Christ. You also need to make that same type of spiritual time with your children. To help you and your family, Harvest Ministries has a number of spiritual resources available to assist you in your relationship with God. You may write to us here at Harvest to receive spiritual resources. You can also receive resources when you register your decision to follow Christ at Harvest Ministries' Web site at www.harvest.org/knowgod. While you're at our Web site, be sure to visit the "Tools for Spiritual Growth" page. There you'll discover biblical teachings and resources that will encourage you as you learn to know God and share His love with your family.

May God bless you and your spouse as you grow closer to Him.

Notes

Chapter Two: God's Plan for Marriage
[1] W. E. Vine, *Vine's Expository Dictionary of Old and New Testament Words*, vol. 2 (Iowa Falls, Iowa: Word Bible Publishers, 1981), 84.

Chapter Three: The Family's Purpose and Plan
[1] Kay S. Hymowitz, "Kids Today Grow up Way Too Fast," *The Wall Street Journal* (October 28, 1998): A, 22.3.
[2] Ibid.
[3] David Elkind, *The Hurried Child: Growing up Too Fast Too Soon*, 3rd ed. (Cambridge, Mass.: Perseus Books, 2001), 52.

Chapter Four: Learning to Live God's Word
[1] The Barna Group, "Born Again Adults Less Likely to Co-Habit, Just as Likely to Divorce," August 6, 2001, http://www.barna.org/FlexPage.aspx?Page=BarnaUpdate&BarnaUpdateID=95 (accessed May 21, 2004).

Greg Laurie
Harvest Ministries
P.O. Box 4000
Riverside, CA 92514-4000

PastorGreg@harvest.org

www.harvest.org

Strengthen Your Marriage
With the Following Titles from Greg Laurie

**(800) 821-3300
or visit our Web site at
www.harvest.org**

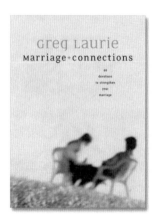

Marriage Connections
Softcover

Clear the communication channels and strengthen your
marriage with these sixty short devotions for married couples.
Pastor Greg Laurie offers sound, biblical principles about
marriage and practical ways to apply God's Word to your own
relationship. Each devotion provides a great starting point for
talking with your spouse about vital connections, such as

- Discovering the secret to staying in love
- Appreciating your differences
- Praying together
- Leaving a spiritual legacy for your family

and much more.

Read Marriage Connections with your spouse and strengthen
your connection with each other.

God's Blueprint for Today's Family
CD Audio Series

Today's family is in trouble. Society is quickly casting aside God's guidelines for family life in order to accommodate today's "me-centered" thinking. In this popular series, Greg Laurie brings us back to God's blueprint for the family with the following messages:

- "What's Love Got to Do with It?"
- "Preparing for a Strong Marriage"
- "How to Divorce-Proof Your Marriage"
- "What the Bible Has to Say to Wives"
- "Four Words That Can Change Your Marriage"
- "How to Get a New Husband"
- "Loving As Christ Loves the Church"
- "A Word to Children and Their Parents"
- "Parenting God's Way"

Highlighting the foundations of a biblical marriage and God's building blocks for parenting, this series will help your marriage not just survive—but thrive. Available on CD or cassette.

Notes

Notes

Notes

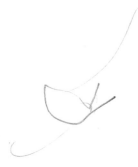